# A Benjamin Blo[g]

## and his Inquisitive Dog

# Guide

# Scotland

Anita Ganeri

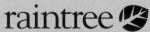

raintree

a Capstone company — publishers for children

Raintree is an imprint of Capstone Global Library Limited, a company incorporated in England and Wales having its registered office at 7 Pilgrim Street, London, EC4V 6LB – Registered company number: 6695582

**www.raintree.co.uk**
myorders@raintree.co.uk

Edited by Helen Cox Cannons and Tony Wacholtz
Designed by Steve Mead
Original illustrations © Capstone Global Library Limited 2015
Illustrated by Sernur ISIK
Picture research by Svetlana Zhurkin
Production by Helen McCreath
Originated by Capstone Global Library Limited
Printed and bound in China by CTPS

ISBN 978 1 406 29090 5
18 17 16 15 14
10 9 8 7 6 5 4 3 2 1

**British Library Cataloguing in Publication Data**
A full catalogue record for this book is available from the British Library.

**Acknowledgements**
We would like to thank the following for permission to reproduce photographs: Alamy: Marcus McAdam, 26; Dreamstime: Creativehearts, 27, Micka, 5, Stevanzz, 11, Tomi Tenetz, 24; Getty Images: Jeff J. Mitchell, 17; iStockphotos: AndrewJShearer, 19, hmproudlove, 21; Newscom: Actionplus/ Craig Mercer, 23; Shutterstock: AdamEdwards, 22, donsimon, 4, 14, Doug Berndt, 16, Elnur, 10, Hector Ruiz Villar, 12, 29, Iain Frazer, 13, Ian Woolcock, 18, James Steidl, 15, John A. Cameron, 8, Jule_Berlin, 6, Paul Cowan, 20, Pearl Media, 9, PromesaArtStudio, 28, Rafa Irusta, 7, Richard Semik, cover, 25.

Every effort has been made to contact copyright holders of material reproduced in this book. Any omissions will be rectified in subsequent printings if notice is given to the publisher.

All the internet addresses (URLs) given in this book were valid at the time of going to press. However, due to the dynamic nature of the internet, some addresses may have changed, or sites may have changed or ceased to exist since publication. While the author and publisher regret any inconvenience this may cause readers, no responsibility for any such changes can be accepted by either the author or the publisher.

Some words are shown in bold, **like this.** You can find out what they mean by looking in the glossary.

# Contents

Welcome to Scotland!. . . . . . . . . . . . . . .4

Story of Scotland . . . . . . . . . . . . . . . . .6

Mountains, islands, lochs and glens. . .8

City streets . . . . . . . . . . . . . . . . . . . .12

*Fáilte*! . . . . . . . . . . . . . . . . . . . . . . . .14

Time for dinner.. . . . . . . . . . . . . . . . . .20

Golf courses and curling . . . . . . . . .22

From oil rigs to fish farms. . . . . . . . . .24

And finally.. . . . . . . . . . . . . . . . . . . . .26

Scotland fact file . . . . . . . . . . . . . . . .28

Scotland quiz. . . . . . . . . . . . . . . . . . .29

Glossary. . . . . . . . . . . . . . . . . . . . . . .30

Find out more . . . . . . . . . . . . . . . . . .31

Index . . . . . . . . . . . . . . . . . . . . . . . . .32

# Welcome to Scotland!

Hello! My name's Benjamin Blog and this is Barko Polo, my **inquisitive** dog. (He's named after ancient ace explorer, **Marco Polo**.) We have just got back from our latest adventure – exploring Scotland. We put this book together from some of the blog posts we wrote on the way.

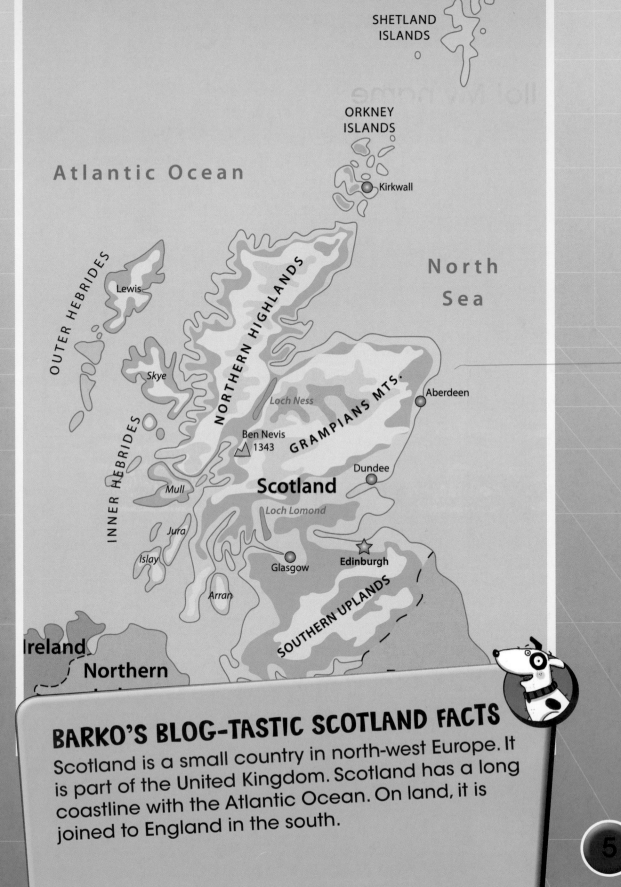

SHETLAND
ISLANDS

ORKNEY
ISLANDS

**Atlantic Ocean**

Kirkwall

**North
Sea**

OUTER HEBRIDES

Lewis

NORTHERN HIGHLANDS

Skye

Loch Ness

GRAMPIANS MTS.

Aberdeen

Ben Nevis
△ 1343

INNER HEBRIDES

Mull

**Scotland**

Dundee

Loch Lomond

Jura

Islay

Glasgow

☆ **Edinburgh**

Arran

SOUTHERN UPLANDS

Ireland

**Northern**

# BARKO'S BLOG-TASTIC SCOTLAND FACTS

Scotland is a small country in north-west Europe. It is part of the United Kingdom. Scotland has a long coastline with the Atlantic Ocean. On land, it is joined to England in the south.

# Story of Scotland

Posted by: Ben Blog | 2 April at 8.46 a.m.

We have come to the Orkney Islands in the far north of Scotland to see the village of Skara Brae. People lived here in the Stone Age, about 5,000 years ago. They lived in stone houses, like this one, which were built partly below ground to keep out of the wind.

# BARKO'S BLOG-TASTIC SCOTLAND FACTS

This is the Wallace Monument in Stirling. It was built to remember the great Scottish hero William Wallace. In 1297, he **defeated** the English army at the Battle of Stirling Bridge.

# Mountains, islands, lochs and glens

Posted by: Ben Blog | 30 May at 12.12 p.m.

From the Orkney Islands, we headed south-west to Ben Nevis. It is the highest mountain in Scotland at 1,344 metres (4,409 feet) tall. The mountain is very popular with walkers and I decided to take a path called the Pony Track to see the large **cairn** of stones on the top.

## BARKO'S BLOG-TASTIC SCOTLAND FACTS

There are hundreds of islands dotted off the Scottish coast. The Shetland Islands are located in the far north. They are famous for Shetland ponies, which are small but very strong.

I'm here in Loch Ness on a monster-hunting trip. This huge lake is 37 kilometres (23 miles) long and up to 240 metres (788 feet) deep. Some people believe that it is home to a gigantic monster, but I haven't seen anything yet. Hang on, what's that dark shape over there?

# BARKO'S BLOG-TASTIC SCOTLAND FACTS

Glencoe is a U-shaped valley, with rocky peaks on either side. Millions of years ago, it was all that was left of a massive volcano. Later, ancient **glaciers** scraped it into shape.

I am here!

# City streets

Posted by: Ben Blog | 3 July at 4.23 p.m.

Edinburgh is the capital city of Scotland and a great place for sightseeing. The first place on my list was Edinburgh Castle, which looks out over the city. This is a snap I took. The castle is built on top of an ancient volcano that stopped erupting millions of years ago. Luckily!

## BARKO'S BLOG-TASTIC SCOTLAND FACTS

This amazing building is the Science Centre in Glasgow. It is covered in metal and looks like the body of a ship. Inside, there are hundreds of science activities and a **planetarium**.

# Fáilte!

Most people in Scotland speak English. Some also speak the ancient language of Gaelic. Many road signs and street names across Scotland are written in Gaelic and English. *Fáilte* means "welcome". There is also a Gaelic-language radio station and TV channel.

## BARKO'S BLOG-TASTIC SCOTLAND FACTS

This man is wearing a traditional Scottish **kilt**. It is made from a type of woollen cloth, called tartan. Traditionally, different Scottish families had different tartan patterns.

Our next stop was the island of Lewis in the Outer Hebrides, where we're visiting a traditional Scottish **croft**. A croft is a small farm where farmers grow crops and keep cattle and sheep. Life on a croft is very tough. Today, most Scottish people live in cities.

## BARKO'S BLOG-TASTIC SCOTLAND FACTS

Scottish children start school at the age of five and stay until they are 16 or 18. Some island schools are tiny, with only two pupils. These pupils attend a big secondary school in Glasgow.

It is New Year's Eve and we're back in Edinburgh for Hogmanay (the Scottish word for New Year's Eve). We're here with tens of thousands of people at a massive street party in Princes Street. The famous firework display around Edinburgh Castle is amazing.

### BARKO'S BLOG-TASTIC SCOTLAND FACTS

In January, the Up Helly Aa festival is held in the Shetland Islands. People dress up as **Vikings** and parade through the streets, carrying torches. The festival ends with them setting fire to a model of a Viking **longship**.

# Time for dinner...

The most famous food in Scotland is haggis, so we thought that we would give it a try. Haggis is made from sheep's heart, liver and lungs, mixed with onion, oatmeal and other ingredients. It is traditionally eaten with neeps and tatties (mashed swede and potato).

## BARKO'S BLOG-TASTIC SCOTLAND FACTS

Cranachan is a traditional dessert, or pudding, that is eaten in Scotland. It is made from whipped cream, mixed with whisky, honey, oatmeal and fresh raspberries, and it is delicious.

# Golf courses and curling

After all that food, we needed some exercise, so we headed to St Andrews. Its golf course is one of the oldest and most famous in the world. Golf was first played in Scotland more than 500 years ago, and it is still very popular today. I'm hoping to get a **hole-in-one**!

## BARKO'S BLOG-TASTIC SCOTLAND FACTS

Fancy a game of curling? It is a Scottish sport where players slide stones along a sheet of ice towards a target. Two of the players use special brooms to sweep the ice and help the stones to slide. Curling is a Winter Olympic sport.

# From oil rigs to fish farms

Posted by: Ben Blog | 14 February at 11 a.m.

From St Andrews, we took the train up the east coast to the city of Aberdeen. It is the centre of the oil industry in Scotland. Oil is one of Scotland's most valuable **natural resources**. Oil rigs, like this one in the North Sea, pump out billions of barrels of oil every year.

## BARKO'S BLOG-TASTIC SCOTLAND FACTS

You can see fish pens, like these ones, in many lochs around Scotland. They are fish farms where farmers keep salmon and trout. The fish grow more quickly than they do in the wild.

# And finally...

Posted by: Ben Blog | 17 March at 2.56 p.m.

Our last stop was the Cuillin on the Isle of Skye. The Cuillin is a range of mountains, with jagged peaks and steep cliffs. The hardest mountain to climb is called the **Inaccessible Pinnacle**. It's easy to see why! The only way to reach the top is by rock climbing. Good luck!

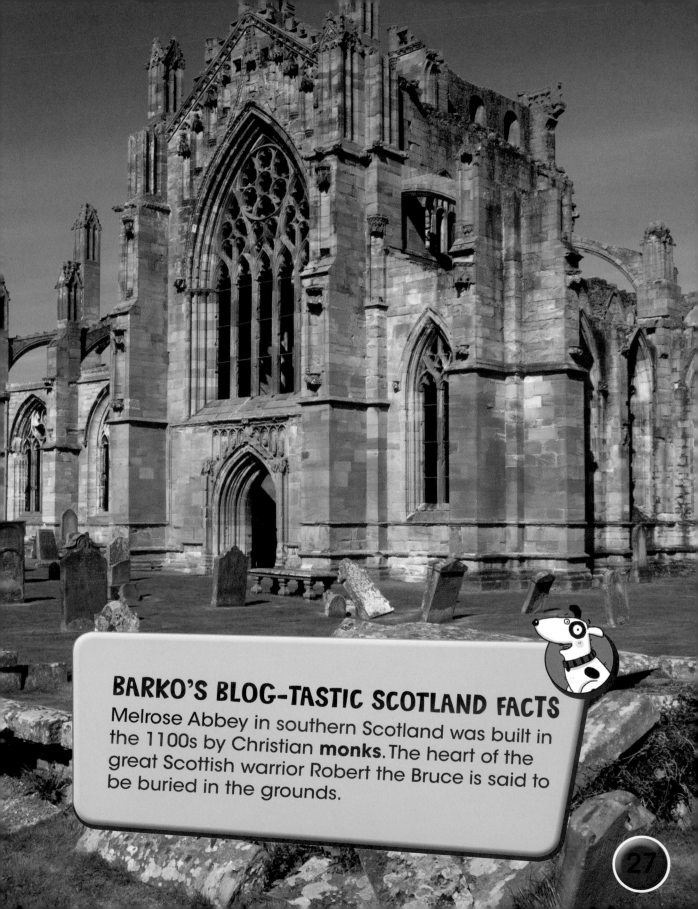

## BARKO'S BLOG-TASTIC SCOTLAND FACTS

Melrose Abbey in southern Scotland was built in the 1100s by Christian **monks**. The heart of the great Scottish warrior Robert the Bruce is said to be buried in the grounds.

# Scotland fact file

Area: 78,772 square kilometres
(30,414 square miles)

Population: 5,327,700 (2013)

Capital city: Edinburgh

Other main cities: Glasgow, Aberdeen, Dundee

Languages: English, Gaelic

Main religion: Christianity

Highest mountain: Ben Nevis
(1,344 metres/4,409 feet)

Longest river: Tay (193 kilometres/120 miles)

Currency: Pound sterling

# Scotland quiz

Find out how much you know about Scotland with our quick quiz.

1. Which is the highest mountain in Scotland?
a) Loch Ness
b) Ben Nevis
c) Wallace Monument

2. Which is the capital of Scotland?
a) Glasgow
b) Aberdeen
c) Edinburgh

3. What is a **kilt**?
a) Scottish clothing
b) Scottish food
c) Scottish farm

4. When is Hogmanay?
a) Christmas Eve
b) New Year's Eve
c) New Year's Day

5. What is this?

# Glossary

**cairn** large pile of stones placed by people on a mountainside

**croft** small Scottish farm

**defeat** beat the other side in battle

**glacier** river of ice that flows from a mountain or sheet of ice

**hole-in-one** in golf, when a player hits the ball straight into the hole

**inaccessible** impossible to reach or get to

**inquisitive** interested in learning about the world

**kilt** knee-length skirt traditionally worn by Scottish men

**longship** Viking warship with oars and a sail

**Marco Polo** explorer who lived from about 1254 to 1324. He travelled from Italy to China.

**monk** man who devotes his life to worshipping God

**natural resource** natural material that we use, such as coal, oil or wood

**pinnacle** very sharp peak or tower

**planetarium** theatre built for watching shows about space

**Viking** person from Scandinavia who settled in Scotland from the late 700s

# Find out more

## Books

*Scotland* (Countries Around the World), Melanie Waldron (Raintree, 2012)

*Scotland* (Horrible Histories), Terry Deary (Scholastic, 2009)

*United Kingdom* (Countries in Our World), Michael Burgan (Franklin Watts, 2013)

## Websites

**kids.nationalgeographic.co.uk/kids/places/find**
National Geographic's website has lots of information, photos and maps of countries around the world.

**www.worldatlas.com**
Packed with information about different countries, this website has flags, time zones, facts and figures, maps and timelines.

# Index

Aberdeen  24

Ben Nevis  8, 28

cities  12–13, 18, 24, 28
coastline  5
cranachan  21
crofts  16
Cuillin  26
curling  23

Edinburgh  12, 18

fish farms  25
food  20–21

Gaelic  14
Glasgow  13
Glencoe  11
golf  22

haggis  20
history  6–7
Hogmany  18

islands  6, 9, 16, 19, 26

languages  14, 28

Lewis  16
Loch Ness  10

Melrose Abbey  27
mountains  4, 26, 28

oil industry  24
Orkney Islands  6

people  14–15, 28

Robert the Bruce  27

schools  17
Shetland Islands  9, 19
Skara Brae  6
sports  22–23

tartans  15

Up Helly Aa  19

Wallace, William  7